Beginner's Guide
to
THREAD CROCHET

by Rita Weiss

Leisure Arts, Inc.
Maumelle, Arkansas

Produced by

Production Team

Creative Directors: Jean Leinhauser and Rita Weiss
Technical Editor: Mary Ann Frits
Pattern Testers: Kim Britt and Tammy Layte
Book Design: Linda Causee

Diagrams © 2014 by The Creative Partners™LLC
Reproduced by special permission

We have made every effort to ensure that these instructions are accurate and complete. We cannot, however, be responsible for human error, typographical mistakes or variations in individual work

Published by Leisure Arts, Inc.

© 2014 by Leisure Arts, Inc.
104 Champs Boulevard, STE. 100
Maumelle, AR 72113
www. leisurearts.com

ISBN: 978-1-4647-1598-3

Introduction

If you have always done your crocheting with worsted weight yarn and a D or F hook, you have been missing one of the great joys of crochet: creating beautiful lace with a steel crochet hook and fine thread.

It's time to pick up your hooks and start working with one of the most beautiful parts of crochet. Even if you have never crocheted before but have admired beautiful lace projects, here is an all-in-one guide to everything you will need to know to become a thread crocheter.

Not only will you find information about hooks and thread, but also we show you how to create the stitches that are the basis of thread crochet. Learn how to increase and decrease in thread, how to crochet in the round and much more.

Finally, when you feel at ease with this new skill, enjoy the 15 easy-to-do projects and test your new skills. Start with colorful coasters and try your hand at the delicate edgings. Make the scarves and shawls, and before you know it, you'll be ready to crochet not only a table runner and matching place mats, but one of the doilies that is crocheted in the round.

BEFORE YOU BEGIN

If you've always admired beautiful lace projects that were created with a crochet hook but didn't know anyone who could teach you how, this is the book for you. Whether you've been crocheting with yarn for years or have never picked up a crochet hook, this is the book for you.

Here, you'll find all the hints and instructions necessary to becoming a thread crocheter even if you have never crocheted before. And, after you've learned all of the techniques, we offer you the instructions for some thread crochet projects ranging from a simple edging to some elegant doilies.

If you've been a crocheter with yarn, you may feel clumsy and awkward at first. You may feel all thumbs all over again just as you felt when you first learned to crochet. However, in a very short time as you work, this feeling will pass as you learn to adjust your tension and method of working with new tools.

One of the great advantages of crocheting with thread is the realization that you won't need a lot of tools. If you wanted to plant a garden instead of just crocheting doilies and scarves, you'd need a lot of seeds, hoes, rakes, shovels and more.

To be a thread crocheter, all you really need is the proper crochet hook, some crochet thread and a tapestry needle.

Crochet Hooks

Thread crochet hooks are tiny hooks that are used to make very fine, lace weight projects, such as doilies and tablecloths. They are designed to be used with thinner threads than regular yarn crochet.

The hooks used most often for thread projects are about 5" long, which is shorter than most hooks used for yarns, and are constructed slightly

differently. These hooks are made from steel which is a harder metal than those used in yarn hooks and is less liable to break at the hook end. This end can be very narrow on the smallest steel hooks. Some steel hooks come with a plastic handle—or you can purchase a rubber handle to place over your steel hook—to make the grip more comfortable, especially when crocheting for long periods of time.

Steel thread crochet hooks are sized differently from regular yarn hooks. In fact the sizing is the exact opposite. The higher the number, the smaller the hook, which is the reverse of yarn hook sizing. Steel thread crochet hooks sold by American manufacturers range in size from 14 (the finest) to 00 (the thickest). Even finer hooks are sold in other countries where much more delicate lace work is often created.

Different countries actually use different numbering systems. Here is a chart which can help clear up any confusion. It shows hook sizes in both the US and the UK.

STEEL HOOK CONVERSION CHART		
Metric	US	UK/CANADIAN
3.5 mm	00	--
3.25mm	0	0
2.75 mm	1	1
2.25 mm	2	$1\frac{1}{2}$
2.1 mm	3	2
2.0 mm	4	$2\frac{1}{2}$
1.9 mm	5	3
1.8 mm	6	$3\frac{1}{2}$
1.65 mm	7	4
1.5 mm	8	$4\frac{1}{2}$
1.4 mm	9	5
1.3 mm	10	$5\frac{1}{2}$
1.1 mm	11	6
1.0 mm	12	$6\frac{1}{2}$
.85 mm	13	7
.75 mm	14	--

Steel hooks are actually engineered to make your work easier and more uniform. To become an efficient thread crocheter, you should know the areas of the hook.

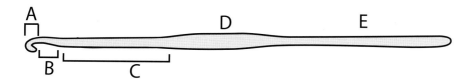

(A) HEAD: This is the "business end" of the hook which will slide in and out of the work as needed. It will grab or hook the thread so you can draw it through other loops of thread (which are the stitches) easily.

(B) THROAT: This is the slanted part from the head to the working area. It helps you to slide the stitch up onto the working area. Never work on the throat or your stitches will be much too tight.

(C) WORKING AREA: This is the most important part of the hook. The stitches are formed on this straight area and then set into their final size. It is important to make certain that all of the stitches are worked well up on this area.

(D) FINGER HOLD: This is a flattened area that helps you grip the hook comfortably by giving you an indented space where you can place your thumb to help balance the work. Stitches should never be formed on the finger hold as they would end up being much too loose.

(E) SHAFT or HANDLE: The part of the hook upon which you rest your hand as you work.

Hold the hook in the right hand (unless you are left-handed), with the thumb and the third finger on the finger hold and the index finger near the tip of the hook.

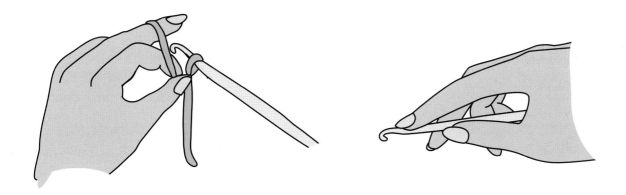

Turn the hook slightly toward you, not facing up or down. Hold the hook firmly, but not tightly. If you are right handed, hold the thread from the ball over the middle finger of your left hand, and hold the hook in your right hand with the thumb and third finger on the finger hold and the index finger near the tip of the hook. If you are left-handed, reverse the placement.

Turn the hook slightly toward you, not facing up or down. Hold the hook firmly, but not tightly.

Crochet Thread

The thread used for thread crochet comes in a number of sizes ranging from a very thin size 100 to a thick size 5. The larger the number, the finer the thread. Size 10, commonly called bedspread weight, is the thread most commonly used (and the one that is used for most of the projects in this book).

Crochet thread is produced by various manufacturers and sold under a number of brand names. The labels on the thread will tell you how much thread in ounces, grams, meters and yards is in the ball. It will also tell you about the fiber content of the thread—usually cotton—and its washability. The label will also give you the dye lot number of the particular ball or skein. The same color—even white or ecru—can vary from dye lot to dye lot. Make certain that all of the thread used for a project is from the same dye lot. Otherwise you may notice variations in color when the project is completed. Other thin yarns are also used to make thread crochet projects such as the ones on page 32 and page 44.

Sewing Needle

A size 18 steel tapestry needle, which is a blunt-pointed sewing needle with an eye big enough to carry the thread as you weave in ends, is necessary for securely weaving in all thread ends.

Gauge

Many new crocheters tend to shy away from gauge as if it were a dirty word. Gauge, however, is the most important word in the crocheter's dictionary. It is the most important lesson a crocheter can learn!

If you don't work to gauge, your finished thread projects may not be the correct size, and you may not have enough thread to finish a project.

Gauge simply means the number of stitches per inch, and the number of rows per inch that result from a specified yarn worked with a crochet hook in a specified size. However, since everyone crochets differently—some loosely, some tightly, some in between—the measurements of individual work can vary greatly, even when the crocheters use the same pattern and the same size thread

The hook sizes given in instructions are only guides. You should never go ahead with a project without making a 4" square to check your gauge. The crocheter has the responsibility to make sure to achieve the gauge specified in the pattern. You may need to use a different size hook than that specified in the pattern. Those hook sizes given in instructions are just guides, and they should never be used without first making a gauge swatch.

Before starting a project, therefore, it is important to make a sample swatch, using the same thread specified in the pattern and the same size hook.

When the swatch is completed, place it on a flat surface without stretching the piece. Now, with a ruler, measure the stitches and rows in the center. If you have more stitches and rows per inch than specified, you are going to need to work the pattern with a larger hook. If you don't have as many as specified, then you need to use a smaller hook. Don't just change to a different hook; start again with a smaller or larger hook and work another swatch.

Sometimes you may find that you have the correct stitch gauge, but you are unable to get the row gauge even with another hook. If so, don't be concerned; the stitch gauge is more important than the row gauge, and if you get the stitch gauge to work, your crocheting will work. The only place where an incorrect row gauge might be a problem is in crocheting raglan sweaters where both gauges must be perfect.

Once you have begun a pattern, it's not a bad idea to check your gauge every few inches. Sometimes if you become very relaxed, your crocheting can become looser; if you become tense, your crocheting can become tighter. To keep your gauge, you might need to change hooks in the middle of a project.

Making gauge swatches before starting a project takes time, and it is a bother. But if you miss this important step, you'll never be able to create beautiful projects.

Finishing a Project

After you have completed your project, you will need to weave in all thread ends.

Thread the tapestry needle with the thread, and weave the running stitches either horizontally or vertically on the wrong side of the work. Start by weaving about 1" in one direction and then ½" in the opposite direction. Make certain that the thread does not show on the right side of the work. Cut off excess thread.

You may wish to wash a project when it is completed. If so, do so by hand, using a mild soap. Rinse it well in warm water, then block it while still damp.

Thread projects have a more finished look when they are starched with a stiffening solution. Commercial stiffening solutions are available at your local craft or needlework department or store. You can also make a stiffening solution from equal amounts of white craft glue and water.

Pour the stiffening solution into a plastic bag, and place the bag in a bowl. After you have washed and rinsed your thread project, immerse it into the solution. Allow the project to remain in the solution for about a minute. Then remove it, and press out the excess liquid. Don't squeeze. The project needs to be very wet, but no solution should be sitting in any of the holes.

Now spread the project out on the flat surface and pin it into shape, using only rust-proof pins. If you are planning to do many thread projects, you might want to invest in a blocking board. Making certain that the right side is up, smooth the project out to its proper size. Make sure that all of the loops and swirls are open and in their right positions. Allow your project to dry, removing the pins only when the project is completely dry. If you cover your board with some plastic wrap before placing the project on it, the completed project will be easier to remove.

Chain Stitch

Most crochet, whether thread or yarn, begins with making a series of chain stitches. The word chain can be confusing in crochet because it is used to mean a single stitch as well as a group of stitches. The chain is the foundation upon which all crochet is built. Think of it as the bottom row of bricks in a brick wall: without that bottom row, there would be no brick wall.

The chain begins by making a slip knot (sometimes called a "slip loop"). Place the end of the thread on a flat surface. Make a loop as shown in **Fig 1**, leaving an end of about 4". The standard abbreviation for chain stitch is ch.

Fig 1

Insert the hook through the center and hook the free end **(Fig 2)**.

Fig 2

Pull this through onto the working area of the hook **(Fig 3)**.

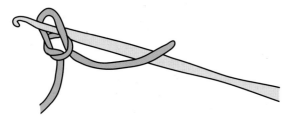

Fig 3

Pull the thread to tighten the knot. It should be snug on the hook, but not too tight so that it slides easily. Be sure to leave the loose thread end at least 4" long to use later **(Fig 4)**.

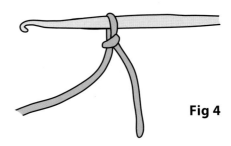

Fig 4

Hold the hook in your right (or dominant) hand and the thread in the other hand and prepare to make the first chain stitch.

Step One

The thumb and index finger of the left (or non-dominant) hand will hold the base of the slip knot with the thread from the ball over the middle finger **(Fig 5)** and under the other fingers of the left hand.

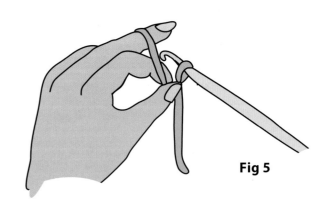

Fig 5

Step Two

Take the thread from back to front over the hook. Catch it with the hook head and draw it through the slip knot on the hook and up onto the working area of the hook **(Fig 6)**.

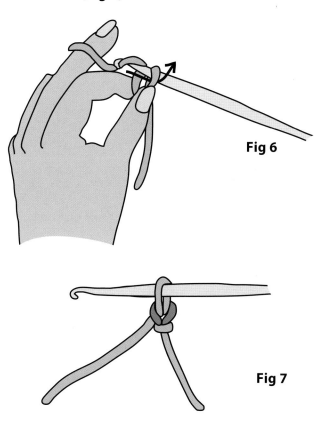

Fig 6

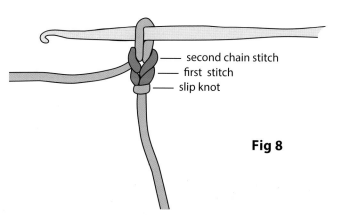

Fig 7

One chain stitch has been completed **(Fig 7)**!

Step Three

Again bring the thread over the hook from back to front, hook it and draw through the loop on the hook (which is the first chain stitch you made).

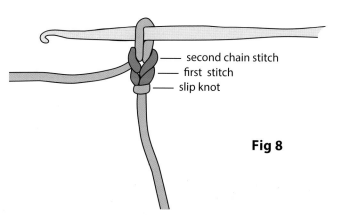

— second chain stitch
— first stitch
— slip knot

Fig 8

Another chain stitch has been made **(Fig 8)**!

In crochet, always take the thread over the hook from back to front, never from front to back **(Fig 9)**.

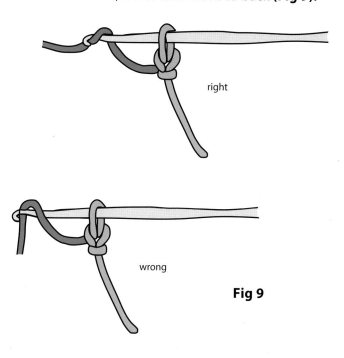

right

wrong

Fig 9

Continue making additional chain stitches in this manner. Don't worry about working too loosely; your chains will become the correct size as you become more experienced. Be sure to work each stitch only on the working area of the hook as shown on page 8. As you work and the group of chain stitches grows longer, keep moving your fingers up closer to the hook after each stitch or two to help maintain control. Here are the right and wrong placement for your fingers **(Fig 10)**.

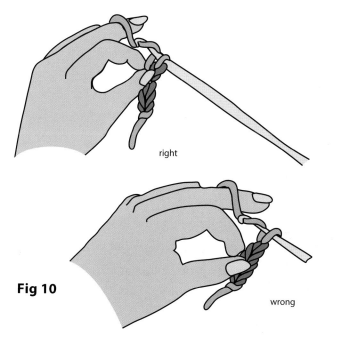

right

Fig 10

wrong

Continue making chain stitches, taking care to take the thread from the back to the front for each stitch and to form stitches on the working area of the hook. The group of chain stitches you are making is called the "starting chain" or the "beginning chain"; these terms always refer to a group of chain stitches.

STARTING CHAIN

Most crochet is worked with variations of four different stitches: single crochet (the shortest), half double crochet, double crochet, triple (treble) crochet (the tallest). The difference is in their height. To work any of these stitches, you will need to make a starting chain, and then work the stitches into it.

Following the steps on page 8, make a slip knot on the hook and make about 10 or 12 chains loosely. Before you begin to crochet a project, you must always very carefully count your chain stitches at the start. Never count the slip knot or the stitch or loop on the hook. **Fig 11** shows how to count.

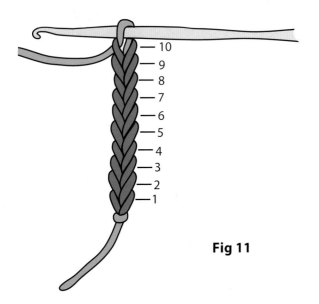

Fig 11

When you look at the completed chain **(Fig 11)**, the front will look like a series of interlocked Vs, each V representing one chain stitch. Turn the chain over, and you will see a row of bumps. Each bump also represents one chain stitch; each V has a corresponding bump **(Fig 12)**.

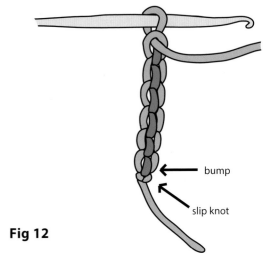

Fig 12

When working the first row of stitches into a starting chain, you will always need to skip one or more chain stitches first, depending on how tall the new stitch will be. You can never work into the very first chain from the hook, as it will unravel.

To work a stitch into the chain, insert the hook from the front of the chain through the center of a V stitch and under the corresponding bump on the back of the same stitch **(Fig 13)**.

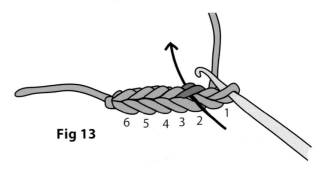

Fig 13

Not including the first stitch, work into every stitch in the chain (unless the pattern tells you to work differently), but not into the beginning slip knot. Make certain that you work the last chain at the end of the row **(Fig 14)**.

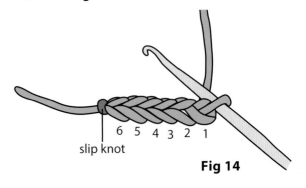

Fig 14

Single Crochet

The shortest and most basic of crochet stitches—and probably the one used most often—is the single crochet. Crochet instructions are written with many abbreviations which helps to keep printed instructions of a manageable length. A list of standard abbreviations and symbols used in most crochet patterns appears on page 23. The standard abbreviation for single crochet is sc.

Row 1 (right side)

Following the instructions for making a starting chain on page 10, make a chain of 6 stitches. Carefully following the instructions shown in **Fig 11**, count to make sure you have 6 stitches in your chain. Hold the 6 chain stitches with the V side facing you, and the row of chains to your left.

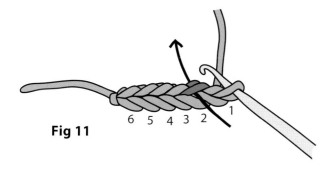

Fig 11

Step One

Skip the first chain stitch from the hook and insert the hook in the next chain stitch through the center of the V and under the back bump. With your left hand bring the thread over the hook from back to front, and hook the thread as in **Fig 15**.

Fig 15

Draw the thread through to the front and up onto the working area of the hook **(Fig 16)**.

Fig 16

Step Two

Bring the thread over the hook again from back to front. Hook the thread and draw it through both loops on the hook **(Fig 17)**.

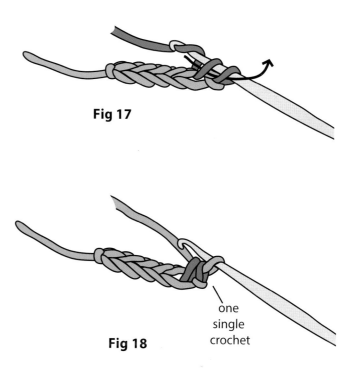

Fig 17

Fig 18

one single crochet

One loop will remain on the hook, and you have made one single crochet **(Fig 18)**!

Step Three

Insert the hook in the next chain as before, hook the thread and draw it though the chain. Hook the thread again and draw it through both loops: another single crochet has been completed.

Continue to work in this manner across the entire chain, taking care to work in the last chain stitch but not in the slip knot. If you began with 6 chains, you should now have 5 stitches in the row. **Fig 19** shows you how the single crochet stitches are counted. As you work, keep all of the V's facing you, being especially careful not to twist the chains.

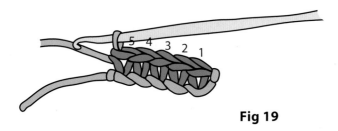

Fig 19

Row 2 (wrong side)

To work another row of single crochet stitches, you will need to turn the piece and work back into the single crochet stitches just made. Whenever you turn the work to start a new row, you will need to first work one or more chain stitches to bring the thread up to the height of the next row. This is called the "turning chain." For single crochet you will need to work only one chain, then turn the chain in the direction of the arrow (counterclockwise) as shown in **Fig 20**.

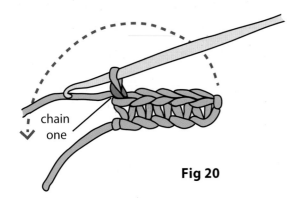

chain
one

Fig 20

Do not remove the hook as you do this **(Fig 20A)**.

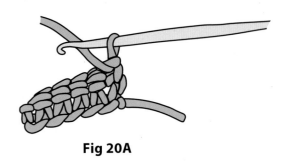

Fig 20A

This **second row**—and all of the subsequent rows of single crochet—is worked into a previous row of single crochet stitches. It is not worked into the beginning chain as you did previously. When you worked into the starting chain, the hook was inserted through the center of the V and under the bump. This is only done when working into a starting chain.

To work into a previous row of crochet, insert the hook under both loops of the previous stitch, as shown in **Fig 21** instead of through the center of the V.

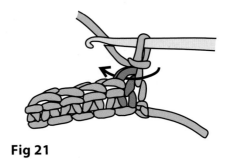

Fig 21

The first single crochet of the row is worked in the last stitch of the previous row **(Fig 21)**, not into the turning chain. Work a single crochet in each single crochet, taking care to work in each stitch, especially the last stitch, which can be easy to miss **(Fig 22)**.

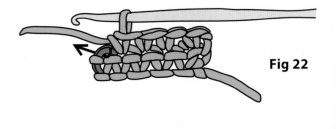

Fig 22

Now is a good time to stop and count your stitches to make certain that you have the proper number **(Fig 23)**.

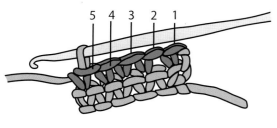

Fig 23

To end Row 2 after the last single crochet, chain 1 for the turning chain, and turn the work counterclockwise.

Row 3 is worked exactly as you worked Row 2. That was easy.

If you wish to practice, work several more rows which means you will repeat Row 2. Try to keep your stitches as smooth and even as possible. Work loosely rather than tightly and make each stitch well up on the working area of the hook. Make certain to chain 1 and turn at the end of each row, checking carefully to be sure you've worked into the last stitch of each row. Count the stitches at the end of each row to make certain that you haven't lost a stitch.

Finishing Off

After working the last stitch of the last row, cut the thread, leaving a 4" end. Draw the loop straight up as in **Fig 24** and draw the thread cut end completely through the stitch.

Fig 24

Double Crochet

Double Crochet is a taller stitch than single crochet. Like single crochet, it also begins with a chain; so chain about 14 stitches loosely, and begin working the first row. The standard abbreviation for double crochet is dc.

Row 1 (right side)
STEP ONE

Bring the thread once over the hook as if you were going to make another chain stitch: from back to front. Skip the first three chains, and then insert the hook in the 4th chain. The loop on the hook does not count as a chain. Make certain that you go through the center of the V of the chain and under the bump

at the back and that you do not twist the chain **(Fig 25)**.

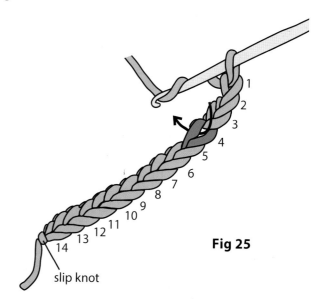

Fig 25

13

STEP TWO

Hook the thread and draw it through the chain stitch and up onto the working area of the hook. You now have 3 loops on the hook (**Fig 26**).

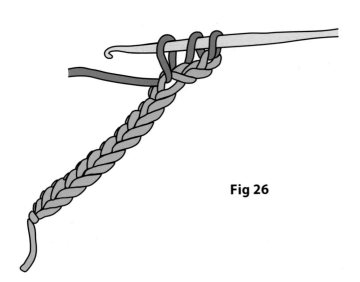

Fig 26

STEP THREE

Hook the thread and draw through the first 2 loops on the hook (**Fig 27**).

Fig 27

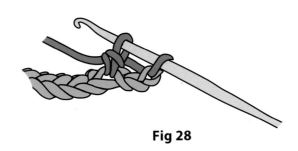

Fig 28

You will now have 2 loops on the hook (**Fig 28**).

STEP 4

Hook the thread and draw through both of the loops on the hook (**Fig 29**).

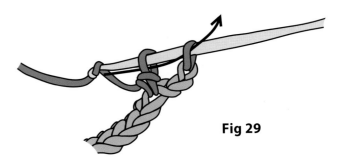

Fig 29

One double crochet has been completed, and one loop will remain on the hook (**Fig 30**).

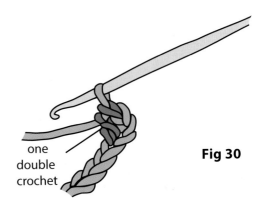

one double crochet

Fig 30

To work the next double crochet stitch, repeat Step 1 but insert the hook into the next chain rather than skipping 3 chains and working into the fourth chain from the hook. Continue in this manner, always working Step 1 into the next chain across the whole row.

When you have worked your last double crochet in the last chain, count your stitches. There should be 12, counting the first 3 chain stitches you skipped at the beginning of the row as a double crochet (**Fig 31**).

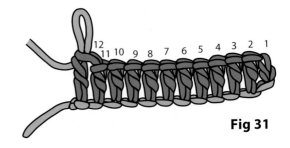

Fig 31

You will need to bring the thread up to the correct height for the next row and then turn the row. Because the double crochet stitches are taller than the single crochet, you will need to chain 3 stitches (called the turning chain); then turn the work counterclockwise before starting Row 2.

Row 2 (wrong side)

The turning chain of 3 chain stitches counts as the first double crochet of this new row. Because of this, you work the next double crochet stitch in the second stitch of the previous row, rather than the first stitch. It is very important to place this stitch correctly. **Fig 32** shows the wrong and right placement for this stitch. Remember that the turning chain always counts as the first double crochet of the row, unless the pattern tells you otherwise.

Continue to work double crochet stitches in each stitch across the row. At the end, work the last double crochet into the top chain of the turning chain of the previous row **(Fig 33)**.

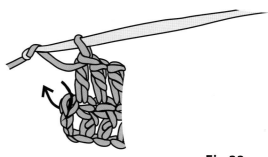

Fig 33

Be careful not to miss this last stitch. Stop and count your double crochets; there should be 12 stitches. Now chain 3 (your turning chain) and turn.

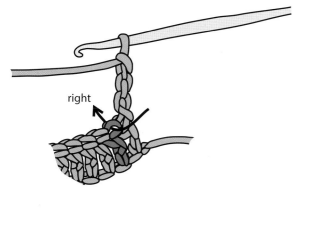

right

wrong

Fig 32

TIP

*Knowing where to insert your hook is sometimes confusing; you must find the top of a given stitch. The V formed by the two loops just to the right of a stitch is the top **(Fig 34)** when working a right-side row and to the left when working a wrong-side row.*

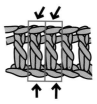

Fig 34

Half Double Crochet

Half double crochet is a versatile crochet stitch that is slightly taller than single crochet and slightly shorter than double crochet. To practice working half double crochet, chain 13 sts loosely. The standard abbreviation for half double crochet is hdc.

Row 1 (right side)

STEP ONE

Bring the thread over the hook; insert the hook through the center of the chain and under the back bump of the 3rd chain from the hook (skipping the first two chains) **(Fig 35).**

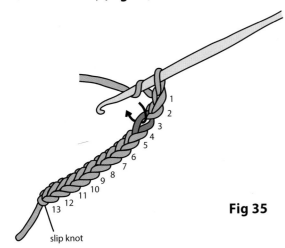

Fig 35

STEP TWO

Hook the thread, draw it through the chain and up onto the hook: there are now 3 loops on the hook **(Fig 36).**

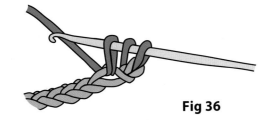

Fig 36

STEP THREE

Hook the thread and draw it through all 3 loops on the hook **(Fig 37).**

Fig 37

One Half Double Crochet stitch has been completed and one loop remains on the hook **(Fig 38).**

one half double crochet

Fig 38

Repeat steps 1, 2 and 3 in each chain across the row, but in step 1, insert the hook in the next chain instead of in the third chain from the hook.

At the end of the row as you did for single and double crochet, you will once again need to bring the thread up to the correct height for the next row by making a turning chain. Chain 2 and turn the work counterclockwise.

Row 2 (wrong side)

Just as in double crochet, the turning chain counts as a stitch in half double crochet. Skip the first half double crochet of the previous row and work a Half Double Crochet in the second stitch **(Fig 39)** and in each of the other stitches across the row. At the end of the row, chain 2 again and turn.

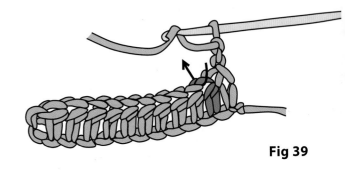

Fig 39

Triple (Treble) Crochet

Triple crochet, often called treble crochet, is a tall stitch that works up quickly. To begin working, make a chain the desired number and begin the first row. The standard abbreviation for triple (treble) crochet is tr.

Row 1 (right side)

STEP ONE

Bring the thread from back to front over the hook twice. Skip the first four chains and insert the hook into the back bump of the fifth chain from the hook **(Fig 40)**.

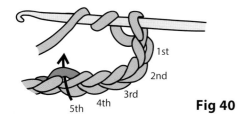

Fig 40

STEP TWO

Hook the thread and draw it through the chain onto the hook; there are now 4 loops on the hook **(Fig 41)**.

Fig 41

STEP THREE

Hook the thread again and draw it through the first 2 loops on the hook **(Fig 42)**.

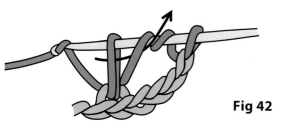

Fig 42

There are now 3 loops on the hook **(Fig 43)**.

STEP FOUR

Hook the thread again and draw it through the first 2 loops on the hook **(Fig 44)**.

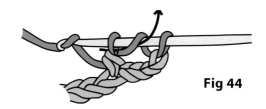

Fig 44

There are now 2 loops on the hook **(Fig 45)**.

Fig 45

STEP FIVE

Hook the thread and draw it through the remaining 2 loops on the hook **(Fig 46)**.

Fig 46

You have now completed one triple crochet, and one loop remains on the hook **(Fig 47)**.

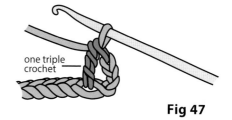

one triple crochet

Fig 47

Repeat Steps 1 through 5 in the back bump of each chain across the row, working Step 1 in the next chain rather than the 4th chain from the hook. Chain 4 (the turning chain) and turn counterclockwise.

Row 2 (wrong side)

The four turning chains have brought the thread up to the correct height and count as the first stitch of the new row. So, remember to skip the first stitch and place the next triple crochet in the second stitch **(Fig 48).**

Repeat Steps 1 through 5 in each stitch across the row, working Step 1 in the next stitch rather than the fourth chain from the hook. At the end of the last row, chain 4 and turn. Remember that the turning chain 4 counts as the first stitch of the new row. Work the next rows as you worked Row 2.

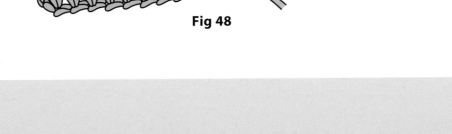

Fig 48

Decreasing in Thread Crochet

Decreases are used to shape a thread crochet piece by eliminating stitches. When the project is worked in a decorative pattern stitch, the instructions will generally explain how to work the decreases. Here are the general instructions for working decreases for the basic stitches.

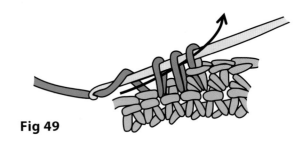

Fig 49

SINGLE CROCHET DECREASE (sc2tog)

(Insert the hook in the next stitch and draw up a loop) twice: 3 loops are now on the hook. Bring the thread over the hook and draw through all 3 loops on the hook **(Fig 49).**

A single crochet decrease is completed **(Fig 50).**

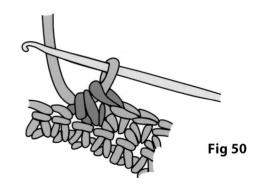

Fig 50

18

DOUBLE CROCHET DECREASE (dc2tog)

STEP ONE

Bring the thread over the hook from back to front; insert the hook in the next stitch and draw up a loop; bring the thread over again and draw through the first two loops on the hook: 2 loops are now on the hook **(Fig 51)**.

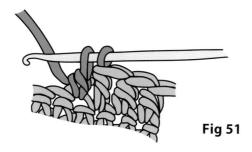

Fig 51

STEP TWO

Keeping 2 loops on the hook, work another double crochet in the next stitch until 3 loops remain on the hook; bring the thread over and draw through all 3 loops **(Fig 52)**.

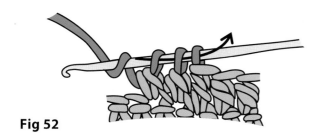

Fig 52

Double Crochet decrease completed **(Fig 53)**.

Fig 53

HALF DOUBLE CROCHET DECREASE (hdc2tog)

STEP ONE

Bring the thread over the hook from back to front; insert the hook in the next stitch and draw up a loop: 3 loops are now on the hook **(Fig 54)**.

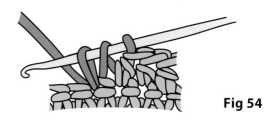

Fig 54

STEP TWO

Keeping the 3 loops on the hook, bring the thread over the hook and draw up a loop in the next stitch: 5 loops are now on the hook, hook the thread and draw through all 5 loops **(Fig 55)**.

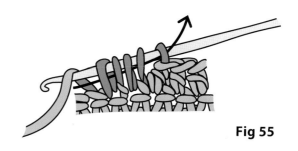

Fig 55

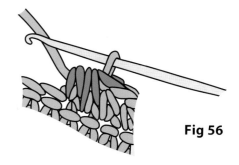

Fig 56

Half Double Crochet decrease completed **(Fig 56)**.

TRIPLE CROCHET DECREASE (tr2tog)

STEP ONE

Bring the thread over the hook from back to front twice; insert the hook in the next stitch and draw up a loop. (Bring the thread over the hook and draw through the first two loops on the hook) twice: 2 loops remain on the hook **(Fig 57)**.

Fig 57

STEP TWO

Keeping these 2 loops on the hook, work another triple crochet in the next stitch until 3 loops remain on the hook. Bring the thread over the hook from back to front and draw through all 3 loops **(Fig 58)**.

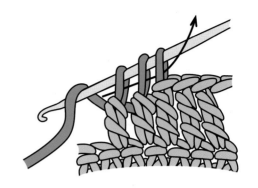

Fig 58

Triple crochet decrease completed **(Fig 59)**.

Fig 59

Increasing in Thread Crochet

Increasing the number of stitches in a row or round is used to shape a piece. In crochet, increases in single crochet, double crochet, half double crochet and triple crochet are made by working two or more stitches in the same stitch. In complicated patterns, methods of increasing are usually given with the pattern instructions.

SINGLE CROCHET INCREASE

Fig 60

DOUBLE CROCHET INCREASE

Fig 61

HALF DOUBLE CROCHET INCREASE

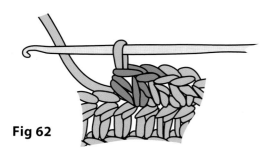

Fig 62

TRIPLE CROCHET INCREASE

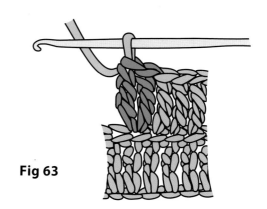

Fig 63

Slip Stitch

This stitch is used in four ways: to move yarn across an area without adding additional height, to join work at the end of a piece worked in rounds instead of rows, to join new yarn and to join seams.

STEP ONE

Insert the hook in specified stitch, chain or loop **(Fig 64)**.

STEP TWO

Bring the thread over the hook from back to front and draw the hook through both loops of the stitch and the loop on the hook: one slip stitch made **(Fig 65)**.

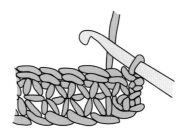

Fig 65

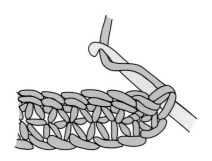

Fig 64

Crocheting in the Round

In addition to working in rows, crochet can also be worked in rounds or circles. Many thread projects are started with a circle.

FORMING A CHAIN INTO A RING

STEP ONE

Make the number of chains specified in the pattern. Then insert the hook through the top loop and back bump of the first chain made (right after the slip knot) **(Fig 66)**.

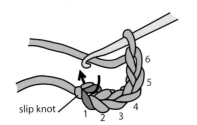

Fig 66

STEP TWO

Bring the thread over the hook (from back to front) and draw through both that chain and through the loop on the hook in one motion. You've now joined the chains into a ring with a slip stitch. Further stitches will be worked into the center of the ring or into the chain stitches of the ring.

JOINING LAST AND FIRST STITCHES OF A ROUND

STEP ONE

Form the ring as directed above.

STEP TWO

Chain 3 (which will count as one double crochet), now work 11 double crochet stitches into the center of the ring. To complete the round, join it by inserting the hook in the 3rd chain of the beginning chain 3 **(Fig 67)**.

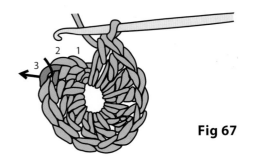

Fig 67

STEP THREE

Bring the thread over the hook and draw it in one motion through the chain loop on the hook, making a slip stitch which joins the round.

Joining New Thread

When joining a new ball of thread, try to make it at the end of a row whenever possible. Make certain that you will have enough thread to complete a row before you start it. Work the last stitch in the row until one final step remains. Then drop the old thread to the back, leaving the loop on the hook. Cut the old thread off, leaving a 6" thread end for weaving in later. Hold the new thread behind the work and complete the last step of the stitch with the new thread **(Fig 68)**.

Fig 68

Make the turning chain with the new thread and continue with it. If you need to change colors in the middle of a row, use the same tehnique, working the last step of the final stitch of the old color with the new color. Cut the old color and continue with the new color.

22

The Language of Crochet
(abbreviations, symbols, terms)

Crochet patterns are written in a special language full of abbreviations, asterisks, parentheses, and other symbols and terms. These short forms are used so instructions will not take up too much space. They may seem confusing at first, but once understood they are really easy to follow.

Abbreviations

approx	approximately
beg	begin(ning)
ch(s)	chain(s)
CL	cluster(s)
cm	centimeter
cont	continue
dc	double crochet
dc dec	double crochet decrease
dec	decrease
dtr	double triple (treble) crochet
fig	figure
g	grams
hdc	half double crochet
inc	increase(ing)
lp(s)	loop(s)
mm	millimeter
oz	ounce(s)
patt	pattern
prev	previous
rem	remain(ing)
rep	repeat(ing)
rnd(s)	round(s)
sc	single crochet
sk	skip
sl	slip
sl st	slip stitch
sp(s)	space(s)
st(s)	stitch(es)
tch	turning chain
tog	together
tr	triple crochet
trtr	triple triple crochet
V-st	V-stitch
yd (s)	yard(s)
YO	yarn over hook

Symbols

*An asterisk (or double asterisks**) in a pattern row indicates a portion of instructions to be used more than once. For instance, "rep from * three times" means that after working the instructions once, you must work them again three times for a total of 4 times in all.

A double asterisk ** and a dagger † are used in the same way as the single asterisk.

: The number of stitches after a colon tells you the number of stitches you will have when you have completed the row or round.

( ) Parentheses enclose instructions which are to be worked the number of times following the parentheses. For instance, "(ch 1, sc, ch 1) 3 times" means that you will chain one, work one single crochet, and then chain one again, three times for a total of six chains and three single crochets.

Brackets and parentheses are also used to give you additional information. For instance, "(rem sts are left unworked)."

Terms

Finish off or Fasten off—This means to end your piece by pulling the yarn through the last loop remaining on the hook. This will prevent the work from unraveling.

Continue in Pattern (Patt) as Established—This means to follow the pattern stitch as it has been set up, working any increases or decreases in such a way that the pattern remains the same as it was established.

Work even—This means that the work is continued in the pattern as established without increasing or decreasing.

Elegant Edging

The perfect trim for a beautiful new project.

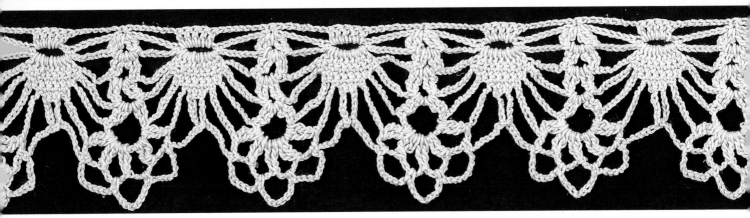

SKILL LEVEL

Easy   ▮▮▯▯

SIZE

Approx 2½" (6.35 cm) wide x desired length

MATERIALS

Size 10 crochet thread 🔟

[100% cotton, 400 yards (365 meters)] per ball

    1 ball ecru

Note: *Photographed model made with Aunt Lydia's® Classic Crochet Thread, size 10 #210 Antique White*

Size 7 (1.75mm) steel crochet hook (or size required for gauge)

GAUGE

18 sc = 2" (5.08 cm)

STITCH GUIDE

Beginning Cluster (beg CL): Ch 4, YO twice, insert hook in specified sp and draw up a lp to height of a tr; (YO and draw through 2 lps) twice; YO and draw through 2 lps: beg CL made.

Cluster (CL): *YO twice, insert hook in specified st and draw up a lp to height of a tr; (YO and draw through 2 lps) twice; rep from * once in same st, YO and draw through 3 lps: CL made.

INSTRUCTIONS

Chain Multiple: 22 + 5

Make a chain slightly longer than desired.

Row 1: In 5th ch from hook work (tr, ch 3, CL); * ch 7, sk next 7 chs, sc in next ch, ch 5, sk next 5 chs, sc in next ch, ch 7, sk next 7 chs, in next ch work (CL, ch 3, CL); rep from * across, turn.

Row 2: Sl st in next ch-3 sp, work (beg CL, ch 3, CL); * ch 7, 9 dc in next ch·5 sp, ch 7, in next ch-3 sp work (CL, ch 3, CL); rep from * across, turn.

Row 3: Sl st in next ch-3 sp, in same sp work (beg CL, ch 3, CL); * ch 9, sc in next 9 dc, ch 9, in next ch-3 sp work (CL, ch 3, CL); rep from * across, turn.

Row 4: Sl st in next ch-3 sp, in same sp work (beg CL, ch 10, CL); * ch 9, sk next sc, sc in next 7 sc, ch 9, in next ch-3 sp work (CL, ch 10, CL); rep from * across, turn.

Row 5: Sl st in next ch-10 sp, in same sp work (beg CL, ch 5) 4 times, CL in same sp; * ch 9, sk next sc, sc in next 5 sc, ch 9, in next ch-10 sp work (CL, ch 5) 4 times, CL in same sp; rep from * across, ch 9, turn.

Row 6: Sc in next ch-5 sp, (ch 9, sc in next ch-5 sp) 3 times; * ch 12, sk next sc, sc in next 3 sc, ch 5, sc in 6th ch of last ch-12 sp, ch 6, sc in next ch-5 sp, (ch 9, sc in next ch-5 sp) 3 times; rep from * across. Finish off.

Edging

With right side facing and beg ch at top, join with sl st in beg ch at base of first 2 CLs, ch 1, sc in same ch; * ch 7, 5 dc in sp formed by next 5 sk chs, ch 7, sc in ch at base of next 2 CLs; rep from * across.

Finish off and weave in ends.

Quick Edging

A great way to practice this new skill.

SKILL LEVEL

Easy ◼◼☐☐

SIZE

Approx 1¼" (3.17 cm) wide x desired length

MATERIALS

Size 10 crochet thread

[100% cotton, 400 yards (365 meters)] per ball

> 1 ball white

Note: *Photographed model made with Aunt Lydia's® Classic Crochet Thread, size 10 #210 Antique White*

Size 7 (1.75 mm) steel crochet hook (or size required for gauge)

GAUGE

18 sc = 2" (5.08 cm)

INSTRUCTIONS

Chain Multiple: 17 + 16

Make a chain slightly longer than desired length.

Row 1: Sc in 2nd ch from hook, sc in next 14 chs; *ch 5, skip next 2 chs, sc in next 15 chs; rep from * across; ch 1, turn.

Row 2: Skip first sc, sc in next 13 sc; * ch 5, skip next sc, in next ch-5 sp work (sc, ch 3, sc), ch 5, skip next sc, sc in next 13 sc; rep from * across to last sc; skip last sc; ch 1, turn.

Row 3: Skip first sc, sc in next 11 sc, * [ch 5, skip next sc, in next ch-5 sp work (sc, ch 3, sc)] twice; ch 5, skip next sc, sc in next 11 sc; rep from * across to last sc; skip last sc; ch 1, turn.

Row 4: Skip first sc, sc in next 9 sc, * [ch 5, skip next sc, in next ch-5 sp work (sc, ch 3, sc)] 3 times; ch 5, skip next sc, sc in next 9 sc; rep from * across to last sc; skip last sc; ch 1, turn.

Row 5: Skip first sc, sc in next 7 sc, * [ch 5, skip next sc, in next ch-5 sp work (sc, ch 3, sc)] 4 times, ch 5, skip next sc, sc in next 7 sc; rep from * across to last sc; skip last sc; ch 5, turn.

Row 6: *Sc in next ch-5 sp, [ch 5, in next ch-5 sp work (sc, ch 3, sc)] 3 times; ch 5, sc in next ch-5 sp; rep from * across to last 7 sc; skip next 6 sc, sl st in last sc.

Finish off and weave in ends.

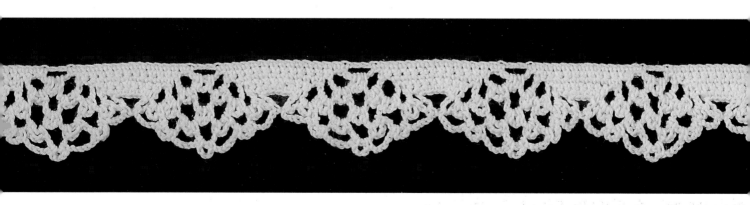

Shells and Clusters

Any simple project will take on added elegance with this trim.

SKILL LEVEL

Easy

SIZE

5" (12.7 cm) wide x desired length

MATERIALS

Size 10 crochet thread

[100% cotton, 400 yards (365 meters)] per ball

1 ball white

Note: *Photographed model made with Aunt Lydia's® Classic Crochet Thread, size 10 #210 Antique White*

Size 7 (1.75mm) steel crochet hook (or size required for gauge)

GAUGE

18 dc = 2" (5.08 cm)

STITCH GUIDE

Shell: (2 dc, ch 2, 2 dc)

Cluster: Keeping last lp of each tr on hook, tr in next 3 sts, yo and draw through all 4 lps on hook.

INSTRUCTIONS

Chain Multiple: 26 + 5

Make a chain slightly longer than desired.

Row 1: In 5th ch from hook work shell; * ch 9, skip next 12 chs, shell in next ch; rep from * across; ch 4, turn.

Row 2: In next ch-2 sp work shell; * ch 3, skip next 4 chs, 5 tr in next ch, ch 3, in ch-2 sp of next shell work shell; rep from * across, ch 4, turn.

Row 3: Shell in next ch-2 sp; * ch 3, 2 tr in next tr, tr in next 3 tr, 2 tr in next tr, ch 3, shell in next shell; rep from * across; ch 4, turn.

Row 4: Shell in next ch-2 sp; * ch 4, skip next tr, tr in next 5 tr, ch 4, shell in next shell; rep from * across, turn.

Row 5: Sl st in next dc and in next ch-2 sp, ch 1, sc in same sp; * ch 14, skip next tr, cluster; ch 14, sc in next ch-2 sp; rep from * across.

Finish off and weave in ends.

The Royal Edge

Add this border to a project, and it's fit for royalty.

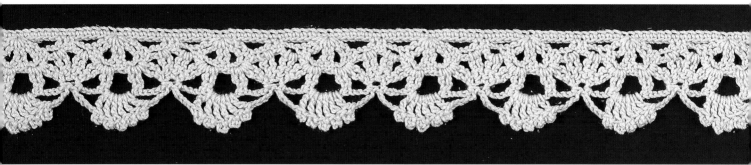

SKILL LEVEL

Easy

SIZE

1½" (3.8 cm) wide x desired length

MATERIALS

Size 10 crochet thread

[100% cotton, 400 yards (365 meters)] per ball

    1 ball ecru

Note: *Photographed model made with Aunt Lydia's®
Classic Crochet Thread, Size 10 #419 Ecru*

Size 7 (1.75mm) steel crochet hook
  (or size required for gauge)

GAUGE

18 dc=2" (5.08 cm)

STITCH GUIDE

Cluster (CL): *YO twice, insert hook in specified
sp and draw up a lp to height of a tr; (YO and
draw through 2 lps) twice; rep from * once in
same sp, YO and draw through 3 lps: CL made.

Picot: Ch 3, sc in 3rd ch from hook: picot made.

INSTRUCTIONS

Chain multiple: 13

Make a chain slightly longer than desired.

Row 1: Sc in 2nd ch from hook and in each rem ch
across; ch 1, turn.

Row 2: Sc in first sc, ch 3, skip next 5 sc, in next sc
work (2 tr, ch 3) twice, 2 tr in same sc; ch 3, skip next 5
sc, *sc in each of next 2 sc, ch 3, skip next 5 sc, in next
sc work (2 tr, ch 3) twice; 2 tr in same sc; ch 3, skip
next 5 sc; rep from * across to last sc; sc in last sc; ch 1,
turn.

Row 3: Sc in first sc, *ch 3, (sc in each of next 2 tr, ch
3) 3 times**; sc in each of next 2 sc; rep from * across,
ending last rep at **; sc in last sc; turn.

Row 4: Sl st in next ch-3 sp, ch 3, tr in same sp; * in
next ch-3 sp work (CL, ch 5, CL); ch 5; in next ch-3 sp
work (Cl, ch 5, CL), CL in next 2 ch-3 sps; rep from *
across, ending with CL in last ch-3 sp; turn.

Row 5: Sl st in next CL and in next 2 chs of next ch-5
sp, ch 1, sc in same sp; * ch 5, in next ch-5 sp work (tr,
picot) 5 times; tr in same sp; ch 5**, sc in each of next
2 ch-5 sps; rep from * across, ending last rep at **, sc
in last ch-5 sp.

Finish off and weave in ends.

Lovely Lacy Scarf

Designed by Lisa Gentry for Red Heart®

A lovely scarf that will be a joy to crochet and then to wear.

SKILL LEVEL

Easy

SIZE

6" x 55" (15.24 cm x 139.7 cm)

MATERIALS

Size 10 crochet thread

[100% viscose from bamboo, 300 yards
(274 meters)] per ball

    2 balls brown

Note: *Photographed model made with Aunt Lydia's®
Bamboo Crochet Thread, size 10 #365 Twig*

Size 7 (1.75 mm) steel crochet hook (or size required
for gauge)

GAUGE

7 Shells = 4" (10.16 cm)

12 rows = 4" (10.16 cm) in pattern slightly stretched

STITCH GUIDE

V-Stitch: (dc, ch 3, dc) all worked in indicated
stitch or space.

Shell : (3 dc, ch 1, 3 dc) all worked in indicated
space

Edging Shell: (sc, hdc, 3 dc, hdc, sc) all worked in
indicated stitch or space.

INSTRUCTIONS

Ch 46.

Row 1 (wrong side): Dc in 4th ch from hook, ch 1,
skip next ch, * V-Stitch in next ch, ch 1 **, skip next 3
ch; repeat from * to last 4 ch, end at **; skip next 2 ch,
dc in last 2 ch; turn: 10 V-Sts, 4 dc.

Row 2 (right side): Ch 3, skip first dc, dc in next dc,
(Shell in ch-3 space of next V-Stitch) 10 times, skip
next dc of V-Stitch, dc in next dc, dc in top of ch-3;
turn: 10 Shells, 4 dc.

Row 3: Ch 3, skip first dc, dc in next dc, ch 1, (V-St in
ch-1 space of next Shell, ch 1)10 times, skip next 3 dc
of Shell, dc in next dc, dc in top of ch-3; turn.

Repeat Rows 2 and 3 until piece measures 53"(134.62
cm) from beginning, ending by working Row 3. Do
not fasten off, but turn to work edging.

Edging

Ch 1, (Edging Shell in corner, and in each ch-3 space
across short side, Edging Shell in next corner and
around each end st of every even row across long
side) twice; join with a slip st in first sc. Finish off.
Weave in ends.

Sea Shell Doily

This elegant doily will suit any decor whether it's modern or traditional, big city or country cottage.

SKILL LEVEL

Intermediate

SIZE

Approx 8" (20.32 cm) diameter with ruffle

MATERIALS

Size 10 crochet thread

[100% cotton, 400 yards (365 meters)] per ball

1 ball white (A)

[100% cotton, 350 yards (320 meters)] per ball

1 ball green (B)

Note: *Photographed model made with Aunt Lydia's® Classic Crochet Thread, size 10 #210 Antique White (A) and #661 Frosty Green (B)*

Size 7 (1.75 mm) steel crochet hook (or size required for gauge)

GAUGE

18 dc = 2" (5.08 cm)

STITCH GUIDE

Beg shell: Ch 3, (dc, ch 2, 2dc)

Shell: (2 dc, ch 2, 2 dc)

Beg large shell: Ch 3, (2 dc, ch 3, 3 dc)

Large Shell: (3 dc, ch 3, 3 dc)

Beg treble Shell (beg tr shell): Ch 4, (3 tr, ch 6, 4 tr)

Treble Shell (tr shell): (4 tr, ch 6, 4 tr)

Double treble crochet (dtr): Yo 3 times, insert hook in specified st and draw up lp, (yo, draw through 2 lps on hook) 4 times: dtr made.

INSTRUCTIONS

With A, ch 4; join with a sl st to form a ring.

Rnd 1: Ch 3 (counts as a dc here and throughout), 11 dc in ring; join with sl st in 3rd ch of beg ch-3-12 dc.

Rnd 2: Ch 3, dc in same ch as joining; ch 2, (2 dc in next dc, ch 2) 11 times; join with sl st in 3rd ch of beg ch-3.

Rnd 3: Sl st in next dc and in next ch-2 sp; beg shell in same sp; in each rem ch-2 sp work shell; join in 3rd ch of beg ch-3. Finish off.

Rnd 4: Join B with sl st in any ch 2 sp; beg shell in same sp; ch 2, *shell in ch-2 sp of next shell, ch 2; rep from * around; join with sl st in 3rd ch of beg ch-3.

Rnd 5: Sl st in next dc and in next ch-2 sp, beg shell in same sp; ch 3, *shell in next shell, ch 3; rep from * around; join with sl st in 3rd ch of beg ch-3.

Rnd 6: Sl st in next dc and in next ch-2 sp, beg shell in same sp; ch 4, *shell in next shell, ch 4; rep from * around; join with sl st in 3rd ch of beg ch-3.

Rnd 7: Sl st in next dc and in next ch-2 sp, beg shell in same sp; ch 5, *shell in next shell, ch 5; rep from * around; join with sl st in 3rd ch of beg ch-3.

Rnd 8: Sl st in next dc and in next ch-2 sp, beg large shell in same sp; ch 6, *large shell in next shell, ch 6; rep from * around; join with sl st in 3rd ch of beg ch-3.

Rnd 9: Sl st in next 2 dc and in next ch-3 sp; ch 3, (2 dc, ch 4, 3 dc) in same sp; ch 7, (3 dc, ch 4, 3 dc) in ch-3 sp of next shell, ch 7; repeat from * all around, join with sl st in 3rd ch of beg ch-3.

Rnd 10: Sl st in next 2 dc and in next ch-4 sp; beg tr shell in same sp; ch 7, * tr shell in next ch-4 sp, ch 7; rep from * around; join with sl st in 4th ch of beg ch-4. Finish off.

Rnd 11: Join A with sl st in ch-6 sp of any shell; ch 6 (counts as a double treble crochet and ch-1 sp), (dtr, ch 1) 15 times in same sp (beg scallop made); sc in next ch-7 sp, ch 1, *(dtr, ch 1) 16 times in ch-6 sp of next shell, sc in next ch-7 sp, ch 1; rep from * around; join with sl st in 5th ch of beg ch-6. Finish off.

Rnd 12: Join B with sl st in first ch-1 sp of any scallop; ch 5 (counts as a dtr), dtr in same sp; 2 dtr in each rem ch-1 sp around; join with sl st in 5th ch of beg ch-5. Finish off.

Rnd 13: Join A with sl st in sp between any pair of dtr; ch 1, sc in same sp; * ch 4, sc in 2nd ch from hook (picot made), ch 1, sc in sp between next pair of dtr; rep from * around, join with sl st in first sc.

Finish off and weave in ends.

Summertime Shawl

Designed by Nazanin Fard for Red Heart®

Just enough warmth for a cool summer evening.

MATERIALS

Size 3 crochet thread
[100% cotton, 150 yards (137 meters)] per ball
  6 balls pink

Note: *Photographed model made with Aunt Lydia's® Baker's Cotton, size 3 #700 Pink*

Size H/8 (5 mm) crochet hook (or size required for gauge)

GAUGE

20 dc = 4" (10 cm) with thread held double

INSTRUCTIONS

Note: *Thread is held double throughout.*

With thread held double, ch 8. Sl st in 6th ch from hook, ch 5; sl st in next ch, ch 3, dc in last ch. Turn.

Row 1: Ch 5, sl st in same ch-space, ch 5, sl st in next ch-space, ch 5, sl st in same ch-space (mark this ch-space), ch 5, sl st in last ch-space, ch 3, dc in same ch-space. Turn.

Row 2: Ch 5, sl st in same ch-space, work (ch 5, sl st in next ch-space) to marked ch-space, ch 5, sl st in same ch-space (mark this ch-space) work (ch 5, slip st in next ch space) to last ch-space, ch 5, slip st in last ch-space, ch 3, dc in same ch-space. Turn.

Rows 3 to 35: Repeat Row 2.

Edging

Row 1: *Ch 1, (dc, ch 5, dc) in next ch-5 space; repeat from *, ending with sc in last ch-5 space. Turn.

Row 2: Sl st in first ch-5 space, ch 3, 4 dc in same ch-5-space, *skip next ch-1 space, 5 dc in next ch-5 space; rep from *, ending with sc in beginning ch 1 of last row. Turn.

Row 3: *Ch 3, sl st in next dc, (skip next dc, ch 3, slip st in next dc) twice; rep from * to end. Fasten off.

Weave in ends. Block to measurements.

SKILL LEVEL

Easy

SIZE

47" wide x 22" deep (119 cm x 56 cm)

Lyric Shawl

Simple but elegant, the perfect song.

SKILL LEVEL

Intermediate

SIZE

Approx 20" (50.8 cm) wide x 64" (152.56 cm long)

MATERIALS

Size 3 crochet thread

[100% mercerized cotton, 150 yards (137 meters)] per ball

      10 balls rose

Note: *Photographed model made with Aunt Lydia's® Fashion Crochet Thread, size 3 #775 Warm Rose*

Size E (3.5) crochet hook (or size required for gauge)

GAUGE

Strip = approx. 3" (7.62 cm) wide

INSTRUCTIONS

First Strip

First Half

Ch 10, join with sl st to form a ring.

Rnd 1: Ch 3 (counts as a dc), 17 dc in ring, join with sl st in 3rd ch of beg ch-3. Turn: 18 dc.

Rnd 2: Ch 4 (counts as a dc and a ch-1 sp), (dc in next dc, ch 1) 7 times; in next dc work (dc, ch 5, dc); ch 1, turn.

Rnd 3: (4 sc, ch 5, 4 sc) in next ch-5 sp; * (sc, ch 4, sc) in next ch 1 sp, 2 sc in next ch 1 sp; rep from * once, (sc, ch 4, sc) in next ch-1 sp, sc in next ch-1 sp, ch 7, turn, skip next ch 4 sp and next 2 sc, sl st in next sc, ch 3, turn; 8 dc in next ch-7 sp, ch 3, sl st in same sp, sc in next ch-1 sp that was previously worked in (sc, ch 4, sc) in next ch-1 sp, 2 sc in next next ch-1 sp, ch 5, turn.

Rnd 4: Skip next ch-4 sp and next 2 sc, dc in next ch 3 sp; (ch 1, dc in next sp) 9 times; ch 5, skip next ch-4 sp and next 2 sc, sl st in next sc, ch 1, turn.

Rep Rnds 3 and 4 until piece measures approx. 32" (81.28 cm).

Last Rnd: (4 sc, ch 5, 4 sc) in next ch-5 sp, *(sc, ch 4, sc) in next ch-1 sp; 2 sc in next ch-1 sp; rep from * 4 times, (sc, ch 4, sc) in next ch-1 sp; working along opposite side of strip, ** (4 sc, ch 5, 4 sc) in next large ch sp, (sc, ch 4, sc) in next smaller ch sp, rep from ** ending with (4 sc, ch 5, 4 sc) to beg of strip.

Finish off.

First Strip

Second Half

With wrong side of work facing, join yarn with sl st to top of ch-3 turning ch of last sp on Rnd 2 of First Half.

Rnd 2: (Ch 1, dc in next st) 9 times, ch 5, sl st in 3rd ch of beg ch-3 of previously worked first half, ch 1, turn.

Rnd 3: (Sc, ch 4, sc) in next ch 1 sp, 2 sc in next ch 1 sp; rep from * once, (sc, ch 4, sc) in next ch-1 sp, sc in next ch-1 sp, ch 7, turn, skip next ch 4 sp and next 2 sc, sl st in next sc, ch 3, turn; 8 dc in next ch-7 sp, ch 3, sl st in same sp, sc in next ch-1 sp that was previously worked in (sc, ch 4, sc) in next ch-1 sp, 2 sc in next next ch-1 sp, ch 5, turn.

Rnd 4: Work Rnd 4 as for First Half.

Repeat Rnds 3 and 4 as for First Half until piece measures same as First Half, approx. 32" (81.28 cm).

Last Rnd: (4 sc, ch 5, 4 sc) in next ch-5 sp, *(sc, ch 4, sc) in next ch-1 sp; 2 sc in next ch-1 sp; rep from * 4 times, (sc, ch 4, sc) in next ch-1 sp; working along opposite side of strip, ** (4 sc, ch 5, 4 sc) in next large ch sp, (sc, ch 4, sc) in next smaller ch sp, rep from **, ending with (4 sc, ch 5, 4sc) to beg of strip. End with sl st in base of previously worked st of First Half.

Finish off.

Second Strip

First Half

Ch 10, join with sl st to form a ring.

Work same as First Half of First Strip to Last Row.

Last Rnd: (4 sc, ch 5, 4 sc) in next ch-5 sp, * (sc, ch 4, sc) in next ch-1 sp, 2 sc in next ch-1 sp; rep from * 4 times, (sc, ch 4, sc) in next ch-1 sp, 4 sc in next ch-1 sp, ch 2, hold previous strip with right side facing and last row at top, working along long edge of previous strip, join with sl st in first ch-5 sp on right edge of strip, ch 2, 4 sc in same ch-1 sp on working

 instructions continued on page 35

strip, (sc, ch 4, sc) in next ch sp * 4 sc in next sp, ch 2, skip next ch-4 sp on previous strip, join with sl st in next ch-5 sp on previous strip, ch 2, 4 sc in same ch sp on working strip**, (sc, ch 4, sc) in next working strip, repeat from * , ending at **, sl st into beg ch of previously worked rnd.

Finish off.

Second Strip

Second Half

Rnd 2: With wrong side of work facing, join yarn with sl st in top of ch-3 turning ch of First Half; (ch 1, dc in next st) 9 times, ch 5, sl st in 3rd ch of beg ch-3 of Rnd 2, ch 1, turn.

Rnd 3: Work as for First Strip, Second Half, making sure to join to the previous strip at the corresponding ch-5 sp by working 4 sc in ch-5 sp, ch 2, sl st in ch-5 of previous strip, ch 2, 4 sc in same sp on working strip.

Rnd 4: Skip next ch-4 sp and next 2 sc, dc in next ch 3 sp; (ch 1, dc in next sp) 9 times; ch 5, skip next ch-4 sp and next 2 sc, sl st in next sc, ch 1, turn.

Rep Rnds 3 and 4 until piece measures same as Second Half of First Strip to last rnd.

Last Rnd: Repeat Last Rnd of Second Half of First Strip.

Finish off.

Work as many strips as will be necessary to have the piece measure about 20" (50.8 cm) wide, following the instructions for the Second Strip.

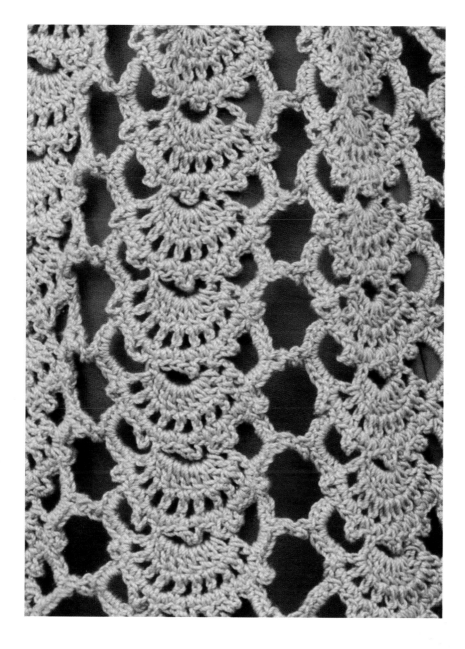

Delightful Doily

A delight to crochet; a delight to use.

SKILL LEVEL

Intermediate ▰▰▰▱

SIZE

Approx 10" (25.4 cm) diameter

MATERIALS

Size 10 crochet thread

[100% cotton, 400 yards (365 meters)] per ball

1 ball ecru

Note: *Photographed model made with Aunt Lydia's® Classic Crochet Thread, size 10 #419 Ecru*

Size 7 (1.75 mm) steel crochet hook or size required for gauge

GAUGE

18 dc = 2" (5.08 cm)

STITCH GUIDE

Triple triple (trtr): YO 4 times, insert hook in specified stitch and draw up a loop (YO, and draw through 2 loops on hook)5 times: tr tr made.

Beg shell: Ch 3, (3 dc, ch 5, 4 dc)

Shell: (4 dc, ch 5, 4 dc)

Beg large shell: Ch 4, (3 tr, ch 5, 4 tr)

Large Shell: (4 tr, ch 5, 4 tr)

INSTRUCTIONS

Ch 4; join with a sl st to form a ring.

Rnd 1: Ch 1, 8 sc in ring; join with sl st in beg sc.

Rnd 2: Ch 3 (counts as a dc here and on following rnds), dc in same st, 2 dc in each rem sc; join with sl st in beg sc-16 dc.

Rnd 3: (Ch 20, sc in next dc) 15 times, ch 10, join with trtr in joining sl st.

Rnd 4: Ch 3, 2 dc in sp formed by joining trtr, ch 4, *3 dc in next ch-20 sp, ch 4; repeat from * around; join with sl st in 3rd ch of beg ch 3.

Rnd 5: Sl st in next dc, ch 3, in same dc work (3 dc, ch 5, 4 dc); *sc in next ch-4 sp, skip next dc, in next dc work shell; rep from * around, ending last rep with sc in next ch-4 sp, join with sl st in 3rd ch of beg ch-3.

Rnd 6: *Ch 5, in next ch-5 sp work (sc, ch 3, sc); ch 5, sl st in next sc; repeat from * around, ending with join with sl st in joining sl st.

Rnd 7: Sl st in next 5 chs of next ch-5 sp, in next sc and in next ch-3 sp, ch 3, 2 dc in same sp; ch 9, *3 dc in next ch-3 sp; ch 9; repeat from * around; join with sl st in 3rd ch of beg ch-3.

Rnd 8: Sl st in next dc, in same st work beg large shell; 3 sc in next ch-9 sp, skip next dc; *in next dc work large shell; 3 sc in next ch-9 sp; repeat from * around; join with sl st in 4th st of ch of beg ch-4. Turn, sl st in next sc, turn.

Rnd 9: Ch 1, sc in same sc, * ch 5, (sc, ch 5, sc) in next ch-9 sp, ch 5, skip next sc**, sc in next sc, repeat from * around, ending last rep at **, join with sl st in first sc.

Rnd 10: Sl st in next 5 chs of next ch-5 sp, in next sc and in next ch of next ch-5 sp, beg shell in same sp; ch 5, * skip next 2 ch-5 sps, shell in next ch-5 sp, ch 5, repeat from * around, join with sl st in 3rd ch of beg ch-3.

Rnd 11: Ch 3, dc in next 3 dc, * in next ch-5 sp work (2 dc, ch 5, 2 dc), dc in each of next 4 dc, sc in next ch-5 sp**, dc in each of next 4 dc, repeat from * around, ending last rep at **; join with sl st in 3rd st of ch.

Rnd 12: Sl st in next dc, ch 3, dc in next 4 dc, * in next ch-5 sp work (2 dc, ch 5, 2 dc), dc in next 5 dc, skip next dc, next sc and next dc**, dc in next 5 dc; repeat from * around, ending last rep at **, join with sl st in 3rd ch of beg ch-3.

Rnd 13: Sl st in next dc, ch 3, dc in next 4 dc, * ch 5, skip next dc, in next ch-5 sp work (sc, ch 5, sc); ch 5, skip next dc, dc in next 5 dc, skip next 2 dc**, dc in next 5 dc; repeat from * around, ending last rep at **; join with sl st in 3rd ch of beg ch-3.

Rnd 14: Sl st in next dc, ch 3, dc in next 2 dc, * ch 5, skip next dc and next ch-5 sp, in next ch-5 sp work (dc, ch 3, tr, ch 3, d c); ch 5, skip next ch-5 sp and next dc, dc in next 3 dc, skip next 2 dc**, dc in next 3 dc, repeat from * around, ending last rep at **; join with sl st in 3rd ch of beg ch-3.

Rnd 15: Sl st in next dc, ch 3, dc in same st, ch 5, * skip next dc, dc in next dc, ch 3, in next tr work (tr, ch 3, tr, ch 3, tr); ch 3, dc in next dc, ch 5, skip next dc, 2 dc in next dc, skip next 2 dc**, 2 dc in next dc, ch 5, repeat from * around, ending last rep at **; join with sl st in 3rd ch of beg ch-3.

Rnd 16: Sl st in next 2 dc, sl st next 5 chs of ch 5 sp; ch 6 (counts as a dc and a ch-3 sp), *tr in next tr, ch 3, in next tr work (tr, ch 3, tr, ch 3, tr); ch 3, tr in next tr, ch 3, dc in next dc, ch 3, skip next 4 dc**, dc in next dc, repeat from * around, ending last rep at **; join with sl st in 3rd ch of beg ch-6.

Rnd 17: Ch 1, sc in same ch as joining; *(4 dc in next ch-3 sp, sc in next tr) 5 times; 4 dc in next ch-3 sp, sc in next dc, sc in next ch-3 sp**, sc in next dc, repeat from * around, ending last rep at **; join with sl st in first sc.

Finish off and weave in ends.

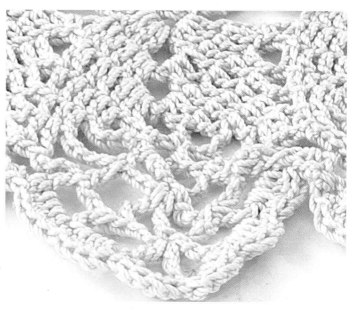

37

Spring Coasters

Designed by Mary Ann Frits

Add charm to any table setting with easy-to-crochet coasters in any color combination you choose.

SKILL LEVEL

Easy

SIZE

4" x 4" (10.16 cm x 10.16 cm)

MATERIALS

Size 3 crochet thread
[100% mercerized cotton, 150 yards
  (137 meters)] per ball
  10 yards (9.144 meters) Green (A)
  10 yards (9.144 meters) White or Yellow (B)

Note: *Photographed model made with Aunt
Lydia's® Fashion Crochet Thread, size 3 #625 Sage
(A) and #423 Maize (B) or #201 White (B)*

Size D/3 (3.25 mm) crochet hook
 (or size required for gauge)

GAUGE

Rnd 1 = 1" (2.54 cm)

STITCH GUIDE

Double Crochet Decrease (dc dec): (YO, insert
hook in specified st and draw up a lp. YO and
draw through first 2 lps on hook) twice; YO and
draw through all 3 lps on hook: dc dec made.

INSTRUCTIONS

With A, ch 6, join with a sl st to form a ring.

Rnd 1: Ch 3 (counts as a dc), work 15 dc in ring; join
with sl st in 3rd ch of beg ch-3: 16 dc.

Rnd 2: Ch 1, sc in same ch as joining, (sc, ch 7, sc) in
next dc (petal lp made); *sc in next dc, (sc, ch 7, sc) in
next dc (petal lp made); rep from * 6 times more; join
with sl st in beg sc: 8 petal lps and 8 sc.

Rnd 3: Ch 1, sc in same sc, (sc, 2 hdc, 7 dc, 2 hdc, sc) in
next ch-7 sp (petal made); *sc in sc between petal lps,
work (sc, 2 hdc, 7 dc, 2 hdc, sc) in next ch-7 sp (petal
made); rep from * 6 times more; join with sl st in beg
sc: 8 petals and 8 sc. Finish off.

Rnd 4: Join B with sl st in 4th st of first petal, ch 5;
*skip next 2 dc, (2 dc, ch 3, 2 dc) in next dc (corner
made); ch 3, skip next 2 dc, work dc dec in next dc
and in 4th st of next petal, ch 3, skip next 2 dc, sc in
next dc, ch 3, skip next 2 dc **; work dc dec in next dc
and in 4th st on next petal, ch 3, rep from * around,
ending last rep at **; to join, YO, draw up lp in next
dc, YO, draw through 2 lps on hook, insert hook in
2nd ch of beg ch-5, draw lp through, YO and draw
through all 3 lps on hook.

Rnd 5: Sl st in next ch-3 sp, ch 6 (counts as a dc and
ch-3 sp); *work corner in next ch-3 sp, ch 3, (dc in next
ch-3 sp, ch3) 4 times; rep from * twice more; work
corner in next ch-3 sp, ch 3, (dc in next ch-3 sp, ch 3) 3
times; join with sl st in 3rd
ch of beg ch-6: 32 dc and
24 ch-3 sps.

Finish off and weave in all
ends.

Table Runner & Placemats

Designed by Mary Ann Frits

The perfect additions for your table, your buffet, or even your dresser.
Make them any length by adding or subtracting motifs.

SKILL LEVEL

Intermediate

SIZES

Table Runner: 12" x 36" (30.48 cm x 91.44 cm)

Place Mat: 15" x 10" (38.10 cm x 25.40 cm)

MATERIALS

Size 10 crochet thread

[100% cotton, 400 yards (365 meters)] per ball

 3 balls for table runner

 1 ball for each place mat

Note: *Photographed models made with Aunt Lydia's® Classic Crochet Thread, size 10 #210 Antique White*

Size 6 (1.8mm) steel crochet hook (or size required for gauge)

GAUGE

Motif = 2⅝" (6.67 cm) square

STITCH GUIDE

Beg Cluster (beg CL): Ch 2, keeping last lp of each dc on hook, 2 dc in st specified, YO and draw through all 3 lps on hook.

Cluster (CL): Keeping last lp of each dc on hook, 3 dc in st specified, YO and draw through all 4 lps on hook.

Shell: 5 dc in specified st.

TABLE RUNNER INSTRUCTIONS

Motif (make 75)

Ch 6; join with a sl st to form a ring.

Rnd 1: Beg CL in ring, ch 3, (CL in ring, ch 3) 7 times, join with sl st in beg CL.

Rnd 2: Sl st in next ch-3 sp, (beg CL, ch 3, CL) in same sp, ch 3, CL in next ch-3 sp, ch 3, *(CL, ch 3, CL) in next ch-3 sp, ch 3, CL in next ch-3 sp, ch 3, rep from * twice; join with sl st in beg CL.

Rnd 3: Sl st in next ch-3 sp, sc in same sp, ch 3, dc in sc just made, *sc in next ch-3 sp, ch 3, dc in sc just made, rep from * around; join with sl st in first sc.

Rnd 4: (Beg CL, ch 3, CL) in same sc as joining, ch 3, (CL in next sc, ch 3) twice, *(CL, ch 3, CL) in next sc, ch 3, (CL in next sc, ch 3) twice, rep from * twice; join with sl st in beg CL.

Rnd 5: Ch 1, sc in same beg CL as joining, *5 sc in next ch-3 sp, (sc in next CL, 3 sc in next ch-3 sp) 3 times**; sc in next CL; rep from * around, ending last rep at **; join with sl st in first sc.

Finish off and weave in ends.

Assembly

Join motifs in 15 rows of 5 motifs each. Sew motifs tog through back lps.

Edging

Rnd 1: With right facing and 1 long edge at top, join thread with slip stitch in upper right-hand corner, working in back lps, ch 1, 3 sc in same st, *sc evenly across to next corner; work 3 sc in corner; rep from * twice; sc evenly across to first sc, join with sl st in first sc.

Rnd 2: Sl st in next sc, ch 1, sc in same sc, *skip next 2 sc, shell in next sc, skip next 2 sc, sc in next sc; rep from * around, adjust reps so that sc between shells is worked in 2nd sc of each rem corner; join with sl st in first sc. Finish off and weave in ends.

PLACE MAT INSTRUCTIONS

Motif (make 24)

Work same as Motif for Table Runner.

Assembly

Join motifs in 6 rows of 4 motifs each. Sew motifs tog through back lps.

Edging

Work same as Edging for Table Runner.

Pinwheel Doily

Remember those sea shells on the beach when you see this lovely doily.

SKILL LEVEL

Intermediate

SIZE

Approx 12" (30.48 cm) diameter

MATERIALS

Size 10 crochet thread

[100% cotton, 400 yards (365 meters)] per ball

1 ball white

Note: *Photographed model made with Aunt Lydia's® Classic Crochet Thread, size 10 #419 Ecru*

Size 7 (1.75mm) steel crochet hook (or size required for gauge)

GAUGE

18 dc = 2" (5.08 cm)

STITCH GUIDE

Picot: Ch 3, sc in 3rd ch from hook: picot made.

INSTRUCTIONS

Ch 8; join with a sl st to form a ring.

Rnd 1: Ch 3 (counts as a dc), 19 dc in ring; join with sl st in 3rd ch of beg ch-3.

Rnd 2: Ch 6 (to count as a dc and ch-3 sp), * skip next dc, dc in next dc, ch 3; rep from * around; join with sl st in 3rd ch of beg ch-6.

Rnd 3: Ch 3, 2 dc in same ch as joining; ch 3, *3 dc in next dc, ch 3; rep from * around; join with sl st in 3rd ch of beg ch-3.

Rnd 4: Ch 3, dc in each of next 2 dc, ch 5, *dc in each of next 3 dc, ch 5; rep from * around; join with sl st in 3rd ch of beg ch-3.

Rnd 5: Ch 3, dc in each of next 2 dc, ch 7, *dc in each of next 3 dc, ch 7; rep from * around; join with sl st in 3rd ch of beg ch-3.

Rnd 6: Ch 3, dc in each of next 2 dc, ch 8, *dc in each of next 3 dc, ch 8; rep from * around; join with sl st in 3rd ch of beg ch-3.

Rnd 7: Ch 3, dc in each of next 2 dc, ch 10, *dc in each of next 3 dc, ch 10; rep from * around; join with sl st in 3rd ch of beg ch-3.

Rnd 8: Ch 3, dc in each of next 2 dc, ch 11, *dc in each of next 3 dc, ch 11; rep from * around; join with sl st in 3rd ch of beg ch-3.

Rnd 9: Sl st in next dc, ch 3, 4 dc in same st; ch 13, *5 dc in 2nd dc of next 3-dc group, ch 13; rep from * around; join with sl st in 3rd ch of beg ch-3.

Rnd 10: Sl st in each of next 2 dc, ch 3; dc in each of next 2 dc, 4 dc in next ch-13 sp, ch 13, skip next 2 dc; *dc in each of next 3 dc, 4 dc in next ch-13 sp, ch 13, skip next 2 dc; rep from * around; join with sl st in 3rd ch of beg ch-3.

Rnd 11: Sl st in each of next 2 dc, ch 3; dc in each of next 4 dc, 4 dc in next ch-13 sp, ch 13, skip next 2 dc; *dc in each of next 5 dc, 4 dc in next ch-13 sp, ch 13, skip next 2 dc; rep from * around; join with sl st in 3rd ch of beg ch-3.

Rnd 12: Sl st in each of next 2 dc, ch 3; dc in each of next 3 dc, *ch 2, skip next 2 dc, dc in next dc, 4 dc in next ch-13 sp; ch 13, skip next 2 dc; dc in each of next 4 dc; rep from * around; join with sl st in 3rd ch of beg ch-3.

Rnd 13: Sl st in each of next 2 dc, ch 3, * dc in each dc to next ch-2 sp, 2 dc in ch-2 sp, dc in each of next 2 dc, ch 2, skip next 2 dc, dc in next dc, 4 dc in next ch-13 sp; ch 13, skip next 2 dc; rep from * around; join with sl st in 3rd ch of beg ch-3.

Rnds 14 to 22: Rep Rnd 13.

Rnd 23: Sl st in each of next 2 sts, ch 3, dc in each of next 2 sts, picot; * (dc in each of next 3 sts, picot) 8 times; dc in next st, in next st work (2 dc, picot, 2 dc); dc in each of next 13 chs, skip next 2 sts**, dc in each of next 3 sts, picot, rep from* around, ending last rep at **; join in 3rd ch of beg ch-3.

Finish off and weave in ends.

Lacy Capelet

Designed by Kimberly K. McAlindin for Red Heart®

Just the perfect coverage for those warm summer evenings.

SKILL LEVEL

Easy ▐█▐█▌☐☐

SIZE

Approx 38" (96.52 cm wide) x 16" (40.64 cm) long

MATERIALS

Fine sport weight yarn

[100% acrylic, 4 ozs, 335 yards (113 grams, 306 meters)] per skein

2 skeins lt green

Note: *Photographed model made with Red Heart® Luster Sheen™ #0615 Tea Leaf*

Size H/8 (5 mm) crochet hook

Size I/9 (5.5 mm) crochet hook (or size required for gauge)

Button

GAUGE

With larger hook, 16 sts = 4" (10.16 cm)

STITCH GUIDE

Foundation single crochet (Fsc): Ch 2, insert hook in 2nd chain from hook and pull up a loop (ch stitch made) *YO and pull through 2 loops on hook (sc made), insert hook in ch stitch and pull up a loop; repeat from * for as many Fsc as called for in pattern.

Cluster stitch: *YO, insert hook in next st and pull up a loop, YO and draw through 2 loops on hook; repeat from * 4 times more, YO and draw through all 6 loops on hook.

INSTRUCTIONS

With larger hook, Fsc 96 sts.

Row 1 (right side): Sc in first Fsc, *ch 3, skip 3 Fsc, sc in next Fsc; rep from * across, ch 1, turn : 24 ch-3 spaces.

Row 2: 2 sc in first sc, *ch 3, 2 sc in next sc; rep from * across, ch 1, turn.

Row 3: Sc in first sc *ch 3, sc in next sc; rep from * across, ch 1, turn: 48 ch-3 spaces.

Rows 4 through 11: Rep Row 3.

Row 12: 2 sc in first sc, *ch 3, sc in next sc, ch 3, 2 sc in next sc; rep from * across, ch 1, turn.

Rows 13 through 30: Rep Row 3 : 74 ch-3 spaces.

Row 31: Sc in first sc, *2 sc in ch-3 space, sc in next sc; rep from * across, ch 3 (counts as dc here and throughout), turn: 223 sc.

Row 32: 2 dc in first sc, skip 2 sc, sc in next sc, *skip next 2 sc, 5 dc in next sc, skip next 2 sc, sc in next sc; repeat from * across to last 3 sc, skip 2 sc, 3 dc in last sc, ch 1, turn: 36 5-dc groups.

Row 33: Sc in first dc, *ch 2, work cluster stitch over next 5 sts, ch 2, sc in next dc; repeat from * across, ch 3, turn: 37 clusters.

Row 34: 2 dc in first sc, sc in next cluster stitch, *5 dc in next sc, sc in next cluster stitch; rep from * across to last sc, 3 dc in last sc, ch 1, turn.

Row 35: Rep Row 33.

Row 36: 3 dc in first sc, sc in next cluster stitch, *7 dc in next sc, sc in next cluster stitch; rep from * across to last sc, 4 dc in last sc.

Finish off.

Edging

With wrong side facing and smaller hook, join yarn at left bottom edge and sc 182 sts evenly up left front edge, across neck edge and down right edge of Cape, ch 1, turn.

Row 1: Sc in first sc, *skip next sc, 5 dc in next sc, skip next sc, sc in next sc; repeat from * across.

Finish off and weave in ends.

Sachets

Designed by Mary Ann Frits

Crochet a bit of luxury: large sachets or small sachets use the same instructions but different weights of thread.

SKILL LEVEL

Intermediate

SIZE

Larger sachet: 4" (10.16 cm) in diameter

Smaller sachet: 3" (7.62 cm) in diameter

MATERIALS

Larger Sachet: Size 3 crochet thread

[100% mercerized cotton, 150 yards (137 meters)] per ball

1 ball white

Smaller Sachet: Size 10 crochet thread

[100% cotton, 400 yards (365 meters)] per ball

1 ball white

Note: *Photographed larger sachet model made with Aunt Lydia's® Fashion Crochet Thread, size 3 #201 White; smaller sachet model made with Aunt Lydia's® Classic Crochet Thread, size 10 #210 Antique White*

Size D/3 (3.25 mm) crochet hook (or size required for gauge) for larger sachet

Size 8 (1.5 mm) steel crochet hook (or size required for gauge) for smaller sachet

Small amount of fiberfill

Scented oil (optional)

GAUGE

Larger Sachet: Rnd 1 = 1¼" (3.172 cm) across

Smaller Sachet: Rnd 1 = ¾" (1.91 cm) across

STITCH GUIDE

Beginning Popcorn (beg PC): Ch 3, 4 dc in same sp; drop lp from hook, insert hook from front to back in top of beg ch-3, pick up dropped lp and draw through lp on hook: beg PC made.

Popcorn (PC): 5 dc in specified sp; drop lp from hook, insert hook from front to back in top of first dc made, pick up dropped lp and draw through lp on hook: PC made.

Picot: Ch 3, sl st in 3rd ch from hook.

INSTRUCTIONS

Top and Bottom (make 2)

Ch 6, join with a sl st to form a ring.

Rnd 1 (Right Side): Sl st in ring, work beg PC in same ring, ch 3; work (PC in ring, ch 3) 5 times; join with sl st in top of beg PC: 6 PCs and 6 ch-3 sps.

Rnd 2: Sl st in next ch-3 sp, work (beg PC, ch 3, PC) in same sp; ch 3, *(PC, ch 3, PC) in next ch-3 sp, ch 3, rep from * around; join with sl st in top of beg PC: 12 PCs and 12 ch-3 sps.

Rnd 3: Sl st in next ch-3 sp, work (beg PC, ch 3, PC) in same sp; ch 3, *(PC, ch 3, PC) in next ch-3 sp, ch 3, rep from * around; join with sl st in top of beg PC: 24 PCs and 24 ch-3 sps.

Rnd 4: Sl st in next ch-3 sp, ch 1, work (2 sc, picot, sc) in same sp, (2 sc, picot, sc) in each rem ch-3 sp; join with sl st in beg sc: 72 sc and 24 picots.

Finish off and weave in ends.

Finishing

If desired, apply scented oil to fiberfill; set aside. Hold Top and Bottom with wrong sides together and carefully matching picots. Sew pieces together below picots, inserting fiberfill before completing sachet.

Turning Chains

When you turn the work at the end of a row, a number of chains must be worked to raise the yarn to the proper height to work the stitches of the next row. Unless you are specified in the instructions, use the following:

For sc: One turning chain; it does not count as a stitch on the following row so the next stitch is worked into the very first stitch of the following row.

For hdc: Two turning chains; the chains count as the first stitch of the following row, so the first stitch is skipped and the next hdc is worked in the second stitch.

For dc: Three turning chains; the chains count as the first stitch of the following row. The first stitch is therefore skipped and the next dc is worked in the second stitch.

For tr: Four turning chains; the chains count as the first stitch of the following row, so the first stitch is skipped and the next tr is worked in the second stitch.

Working Into the Starting Chains

For sc: Work in the 2nd ch from the hook. The skipped chains do not count as a stitch. Make one more chain than the final number of stitches needed.

For hdc: Work in the 3rd chain from the hook. The skipped chains count as a stitch. Make two more chains than the final number of stitches needed.

For dc: Work in the 4th chain from the hook. The skipped chains count as a stitch. Make two more chains than the final number of stitches needed.

For tr: Work in the 5th chain from the hook. The skipped chains count as a stitch. Make three more chains than the final number of stitches needed.

Crochet Terminology

The patterns in this book have been written using the crochet terminology that is used in the United States. Terms which may have different equivalents in other parts of the world are listed below.

UNITED STATES	INTERNATIONAL
Double crochet (dc)	treble crochet (tr)
Gauge	tension
Half double crochet (hdc)	half treble crochet (htr)
Single crochet (sc)	double crochet
Skip	miss
Slip stitch	single crochet
Triple crochet (tr)	double treble crochet (dtr)

Standard Yarn Weights

To make it easier for yarn manufacturers, publishers, and designers to prepare consumer-friendly products and for consumers to select the right materials for a project, the following standard yarn weight system has been adopted.

Categories of yarn, gauge, ranges, and recommended hook sizes

Yarn Weight Symbol & Category Names	0 Lace	1 Super Fine	2 Fine	3 Light	4 Medium	5 Bulky	6 Super Bulky
Type of Yarns in Category	Fingering 10 count crochet	Sock Fingering, Baby	Sport, Baby	DK, Light, Worsted	Worsted, Afghan, Aran	Chunky, Craft, Rug	Bulky, Roving
Crochet Gauge* Ranges in Single Crochet to 4 inch	32-42 sts*	21-32 sts	16-20 sts	12-17 sts	11-14 sts	8-11 sts	5-9 sts
Recommended Hook in Metric Size Range	Steel** 1.6-1.4mm Regular Hook 2.25mm	2.25-3.5mm	3.5-4.5mm	4.5-5.5mm	5.5-6.5mm	6.5-9mm	9mm and larger
Recommended Hook in US Size Range	Steel** 6, 7, 8	B-1 to E-4	E-4 to 7	7 to I-9	I-9 to K-10.5	K-10.5 to M-13	M-13 and larger

*Lace weight yarns are usually crocheted on larger hooks to create lacy, openwork patterns. Accordingly, a gauge range is difficult to determine. Always follow the gauge stated in your pattern.
** Steel crochet hooks are sized differently from regular hooks—the higher the number, the smaller the hook, which is the reverse of regular hook sizing.

Skill Levels

Yarn manufacturers, publishers, needle and hook manufacturers have worked together to set up a series of guidelines and symbols to bring uniformity to patterns. Before beginning a project, check to see if your skill level is equal to the one listed for the project.

Beginner Projects for first-time crocheters using basic stitches and minimal shaping.

Easy Projects using yarn with basic stitches, repetitive stitch patterns, simple color changes, and simple shaping and finishing.

Intermediate Projects using a variety of techniques, such as basic lace patterns or color patterns, mid-level shaping and finishing.

Experienced Projects with intricate stitch patterns, techniques and dimension, such as non-repeating patterns, multi-color techniques, fine threads, small hooks, detailed shaping and refined finishing.